Amyloidosis Guide

The Importance of Early Detection of Amyloidosis

By

Malcolm Oistin
Copyright@2023

Table of Contents

CHAPTER 1 5

Introduction 5

   1.1 What is Amyloidosis? 5

   1.2 Types of Amyloidosis 7

   1.3 Causes and Risk Factors 10

CHAPTER 2 14

Understanding Amyloid Proteins 14

   2.1 What are Amyloid Proteins? .. 14

   2.2 Formation of Amyloid Fibrils 16

   2.3 How Amyloidosis Affects the Body 18

CHAPTER 3 21

Common Symptoms and Signs 21

   3.1 Recognizing Amyloidosis Symptoms 21

   3.2 Diagnostic Challenges 24

3.3 When to Seek Medical Help...26

CHAPTER 4 29

Diagnosing Amyloidosis 29

4.1 Medical History and Physical Examination 29

4.2 Laboratory Tests.....................32

4.3 Imaging and Biopsy Procedures 37

CHAPTER 5 43

Types of Amyloidosis......................43

5.1 Systemic Amyloidosis............43

5.2 Localized Amyloidosis...........48

5.3 Hereditary Amyloidosis 52

CHAPTER 6 57

Treatment Options 57

6.1 Managing Amyloidosis 57

6.2 Medications and Therapies for Amyloidosis 64

6.3 Potential Complications of Amyloidosis 70

6.4 Coping Strategies for Living with Amyloidosis 76

6.5 The Importance of Early Detection of Amyloidosis.............82

CHAPTER 1

Introduction

1.1 What is Amyloidosis?

Amyloidosis is a rare but serious medical condition characterized by the abnormal accumulation of misfolded proteins known as amyloid fibrils. These amyloid fibrils can deposit in various tissues and organs throughout the body, disrupting their normal function. The name "amyloidosis" is derived from the Greek word "amyloidos," meaning "starchy," which reflects the starch-like appearance of these protein deposits when viewed under a microscope.

The primary feature of amyloidosis is the aggregation of these abnormal proteins, which can accumulate in vital organs such as the heart, kidneys, liver, spleen, and nervous system. This accumulation gradually impairs the organ's function, leading to a range of symptoms and potential complications, which can be life-threatening if not properly managed.

There are several types of amyloidosis, each associated with distinct protein variants, organ involvement, and clinical presentations. The type and severity of amyloidosis can vary widely among individuals, making diagnosis and treatment challenging.

1.2 Types of Amyloidosis

There are several recognized types of amyloidosis, each associated with specific protein precursors:

1. **AL Amyloidosis (Immunoglobulin Light Chain Amyloidosis)**: This is the most common type of amyloidosis and is associated with the abnormal deposition of immunoglobulin light chains, which are components of antibodies produced by plasma cells. AL amyloidosis primarily affects the heart, kidneys, and nervous system and is often associated with plasma cell disorders like multiple myeloma.

2. **AA Amyloidosis (Amyloid A Amyloidosis)**: AA amyloidosis

is linked to the accumulation of amyloid A protein and is usually a secondary response to chronic inflammatory conditions such as rheumatoid arthritis, Crohn's disease, or tuberculosis. It typically affects the kidneys, liver, and spleen.

3. **ATTR Amyloidosis (Transthyretin Amyloidosis)**: ATTR amyloidosis is caused by the aggregation of transthyretin (TTR) protein, which is primarily produced by the liver. It can be hereditary (hATTR) or acquired (wild-type or senile systemic). ATTR amyloidosis predominantly affects the heart, nervous system, and gastrointestinal tract.

4. **AApoAI and AApAII Amyloidosis**: These are rare

forms of amyloidosis caused by mutations in apolipoprotein AI (AApoAI) or apolipoprotein AII (AApoAII). They can result in cardiac and kidney involvement, respectively.

5. **Localized Amyloidosis**: Unlike systemic forms of amyloidosis, localized amyloidosis is limited to a specific organ or tissue. Common sites for localized amyloidosis include the skin, respiratory tract, gastrointestinal tract, and urinary bladder.

6. **Senile Systemic Amyloidosis**: This type of amyloidosis typically affects the heart and is more common in older individuals. It is associated with the deposition of TTR amyloid.

Understanding the specific type of amyloidosis is crucial for diagnosis and treatment, as different types may require different approaches to manage the disease and its associated complications.

1.3 Causes and Risk Factors

The causes of amyloidosis are primarily related to the abnormal production and deposition of amyloid proteins. While the exact mechanisms triggering this misfolding are not always clear, several risk factors and associations have been identified:

1. **Plasma Cell Disorders**: Conditions such as multiple myeloma and monoclonal gammopathy of undetermined

significance (MGUS) are closely linked to AL amyloidosis.

2. **Chronic Inflammatory Diseases**: Persistent inflammation from conditions like rheumatoid arthritis, inflammatory bowel disease, or chronic infections can lead to AA amyloidosis.

3. **Hereditary Factors**: Some forms of amyloidosis, such as hATTR and familial forms of AApoAI and AApoAII, have a genetic basis and can be passed down through families.

4. **Age**: Senile systemic amyloidosis, associated with TTR deposition in the heart, primarily affects older individuals.

5. **Gender**: Some types of amyloidosis may have gender predilections. For example, hATTR amyloidosis is often more severe in males.

6. **Ethnicity**: Certain forms of amyloidosis have a higher prevalence in specific ethnic groups.

7. **Environmental Factors**: Exposure to environmental toxins or substances that affect protein folding may contribute to amyloidosis in some cases.

Understanding these causes and risk factors is essential for early diagnosis and intervention, as it can help identify individuals at higher risk and guide appropriate screening and monitoring strategies.

amyloidosis is a diverse group of diseases characterized by the accumulation of misfolded proteins in various organs and tissues. The specific type of amyloidosis and its associated risk factors play a crucial role in determining the course of the disease and its management. Developing a comprehensive understanding of amyloidosis is the first step toward effective diagnosis and treatment.

CHAPTER 2

Understanding Amyloid Proteins

2.1 What are Amyloid Proteins?

Amyloid proteins are a key player in the development of amyloidosis. They are typically soluble, functional proteins that, due to various factors, misfold and aggregate into insoluble, fibrous structures known as amyloid fibrils. These amyloid fibrils are the hallmark of amyloidosis and are responsible for the disruption of normal tissue and organ function.

Amyloid proteins can vary depending on the type of amyloidosis. For example:

- In AL amyloidosis, amyloid proteins are often derived from immunoglobulin light chains produced by plasma cells.

- In AA amyloidosis, they are derived from the acute-phase protein serum amyloid A (SAA).

- In ATTR amyloidosis, transthyretin (TTR) is the primary amyloidogenic protein.

The exact mechanism by which these proteins misfold and aggregate is not fully understood, but it is thought to involve genetic mutations, environmental factors, or changes in protein stability and metabolism. These misfolded proteins are resistant to normal cellular degradation processes and accumulate over time, causing damage to surrounding tissues and organs.

2.2 Formation of Amyloid Fibrils

The formation of amyloid fibrils is a complex process that involves the transformation of normally soluble proteins into insoluble, beta-sheet-rich structures. This transformation leads to the characteristic amyloid deposits seen in amyloidosis.

The process generally involves several stages:

- **Protein Misfolding**: Underlying factors, such as genetic mutations or environmental triggers, cause the amyloid proteins to misfold.

- **Oligomerization**: Misfolded proteins aggregate into small, toxic oligomers. These oligomers have been implicated in cellular damage and the pathogenesis of amyloidosis.

- **Fibril Formation**: Oligomers further assemble into longer, insoluble fibrils. These fibrils are stable, highly organized, and resistant to degradation.

- **Deposition**: The amyloid fibrils deposit in tissues and organs, often interfering with their normal structure and function.

The precise details of these steps can vary between different types of amyloidosis and may involve different proteins and pathways. This complexity highlights the challenges in understanding and treating amyloidosis.

2.3 How Amyloidosis Affects the Body

Amyloidosis can have a wide-ranging impact on the body, depending on the type of amyloidosis and the organs affected. The primary consequences of amyloidosis include:

- **Organ Dysfunction**: The progressive deposition of amyloid fibrils disrupts the normal function of affected organs. This dysfunction can lead to symptoms and complications specific to the affected organ, such as heart failure in cardiac amyloidosis or kidney damage in renal amyloidosis.

- **Symptoms**: Symptoms of amyloidosis can be diverse and may include fatigue, shortness of breath, weight loss, edema (fluid retention), neuropathy (nerve damage), and more. The specific symptoms are often related to the organs involved.

- **Complications**: Amyloidosis can lead to serious complications, including cardiac arrhythmias, kidney failure, gastrointestinal problems, and peripheral neuropathy.

- **Prognosis**: The prognosis for amyloidosis varies widely based on the type and extent of organ involvement. Some forms of amyloidosis are more treatable than others, and early diagnosis is crucial for better outcomes.

amyloid proteins play a central role in amyloidosis, with the misfolding and aggregation of these proteins leading to the formation of amyloid fibrils. These fibrils, once deposited in organs and tissues, disrupt normal function and can result in a wide range of symptoms and complications. Understanding the mechanisms behind amyloid formation and its impact on the body is essential for both diagnosis and treatment of amyloidosis.

CHAPTER 3

Common Symptoms and Signs

Amyloidosis can present with a wide array of symptoms, and recognizing them is crucial for early diagnosis and management.

3.1 Recognizing Amyloidosis Symptoms

Recognizing the symptoms of amyloidosis can be challenging because they often mimic those of other more common conditions. Additionally, the symptoms can vary depending on the type of amyloidosis and the affected organs. Some of the common symptoms and signs of amyloidosis include:

- **Fatigue**: Persistent tiredness and lack of energy are common early signs of amyloidosis.

- **Edema**: Swelling, especially around the ankles and legs, is a common symptom due to fluid retention caused by kidney involvement.

- **Shortness of Breath**: Cardiac amyloidosis can lead to heart failure and symptoms such as shortness of breath, palpitations, and chest pain.

- **Unexplained Weight Loss**: Significant and unexplained weight loss may occur in some cases of amyloidosis.

- **Neuropathy**: Nerve damage can result in symptoms like numbness, tingling, weakness, and difficulty with fine motor skills.

- **Gastrointestinal Symptoms**: These may include diarrhea, constipation, and malabsorption issues.

- **Easy Bruising**: Amyloidosis can lead to abnormal bleeding or bruising.

- **Enlarged Organs**: Enlarged liver and spleen (hepatosplenomegaly) can be a sign of systemic amyloidosis.

- **Skin Changes**: Some forms of amyloidosis can cause skin lesions or nodules.

- **Hoarseness**: Amyloid deposits in the throat or vocal cords can lead to voice changes.

The severity and combination of these symptoms can vary widely between individuals. Due to this variability and the overlap with other medical conditions, amyloidosis is often misdiagnosed or diagnosed late.

3.2 Diagnostic Challenges

Diagnosing amyloidosis can be challenging for several reasons:

- **Symptoms Mimic Other Conditions**: Many amyloidosis symptoms are non-specific and resemble those of other, more common disorders. This can lead to misdiagnosis or delayed diagnosis.

- **Rare Disease**: Amyloidosis is considered a rare disease, and many healthcare professionals may not encounter it frequently, making it less familiar for them.

- **Multiple Organ Involvement**: Different types of amyloidosis can affect various organs, and multiple organ involvement can complicate diagnosis.

- **Non-Invasive Testing**: Traditional diagnostic methods like biopsies may not be suitable for some individuals, as obtaining samples from affected organs can be invasive and risky.

- **Varied Presentation**: Amyloidosis can have a highly variable presentation, even within the same type, making it challenging to establish a definitive diagnosis.

3.3 When to Seek Medical Help

Given the diagnostic challenges and the potential seriousness of amyloidosis, it's crucial to seek medical attention if you experience any of the symptoms mentioned above, particularly if they are persistent, unexplained, or worsening over time. Additionally:

- If you have a family history of amyloidosis or are aware of a genetic mutation associated with the disease, it's important to inform your healthcare provider.

- If you have been diagnosed with a condition known to be associated with secondary (AA) amyloidosis, such as chronic inflammatory diseases, regular monitoring is essential.

- If you have been diagnosed with multiple myeloma and experience symptoms like edema, fatigue, or unexplained weight loss, you should discuss the possibility of AL amyloidosis with your healthcare provider.

Early diagnosis of amyloidosis is critical, as it allows for prompt treatment, which can help slow the progression of the disease and reduce the risk of severe organ damage. Medical professionals may use a combination of physical exams, blood tests, imaging, and tissue biopsies to diagnose amyloidosis. If you suspect you may have amyloidosis or are at risk, it is essential to seek expert medical evaluation and consultation.

CHAPTER 4

Diagnosing Amyloidosis

Diagnosing amyloidosis can be a complex process due to the variability of symptoms and the rarity of the condition.

4.1 Medical History and Physical Examination

Medical History:

- **Patient Interview**: The diagnostic process often begins with a detailed interview with the patient. During this discussion, the healthcare provider will inquire about the patient's symptoms, their onset, duration, and progression. Specific questions may be asked about any family history of amyloidosis or known genetic mutations associated with the disease.

- **Underlying Conditions**: Information about any underlying diseases or conditions, such as multiple myeloma or chronic inflammatory diseases, is crucial, as these can be associated with secondary (AA) amyloidosis.

- **Medications**: The patient's medication history is relevant, as certain medications may contribute to the development of amyloidosis.

- **Family History**: A thorough family history can help identify any potential genetic predisposition to amyloidosis.

Physical Examination:

- **Edema**: The presence of edema, especially in the lower extremities, may be noted during a physical examination. Edema is a common symptom associated with amyloidosis.

- **Skin Changes**: Skin lesions or nodules may be observed, particularly in localized amyloidosis.

- **Enlarged Organs**: The provider may check for

hepatosplenomegaly, or enlargement of the liver and spleen, which can be a sign of systemic amyloidosis.

- **Voice Changes**: If there are deposits in the throat or vocal cords, voice changes or hoarseness may be noticeable.

- **Neurological Assessment**: If neuropathy is suspected, a neurological assessment, including sensory and motor function, may be conducted.

4.2 Laboratory Tests

Laboratory tests are an essential component of the diagnostic process for amyloidosis. These tests aim to identify abnormal protein deposition and its underlying cause. Key laboratory tests include:

- **Serum and Urine Protein Electrophoresis**: These tests are used to assess the presence of abnormal proteins in the blood and urine. In AL amyloidosis, a monoclonal protein spike may be detected in the electrophoresis. This can be a clue that the patient has a plasma cell disorder, such as multiple myeloma.

- **Immunofixation Electrophoresis**: This test can help identify the specific type of abnormal immunoglobulin light chain in AL amyloidosis.

- **Free Light Chain Assay**: Measures the levels of free immunoglobulin light chains in the blood. Elevated levels can suggest AL amyloidosis.

- **Complete Blood Count (CBC)**: This test can identify abnormalities such as anemia, which may be present in some cases of amyloidosis.

- **Kidney Function Tests**: Blood and urine tests are performed to assess kidney function. Proteinuria (the presence of excess protein in the urine) can be a sign of kidney involvement.

- **Liver Function Tests**: These tests assess the function of the liver and may reveal abnormalities associated with hepatic involvement in amyloidosis.

- **N-terminal pro-brain natriuretic peptide (NT-proBNP) and Troponin**: These markers are useful for assessing heart involvement, especially in cardiac amyloidosis.

- **Genetic Testing**: In cases of hereditary amyloidosis, genetic testing may be recommended to identify specific mutations associated with the condition.

- **Tissue Biopsy**: While laboratory tests are valuable, a definitive diagnosis often requires a tissue biopsy. This involves obtaining a small sample of the affected tissue, such as fat, skin, or an organ, and examining it under a microscope to confirm the presence of amyloid deposits.

The specific type of amyloid can be determined through immunohistochemistry.

- **Bone Marrow Biopsy**: In some cases, a bone marrow biopsy may be performed to assess for underlying plasma cell disorders associated with AL amyloidosis.

These laboratory tests play a crucial role in diagnosing amyloidosis and determining the type and extent of the disease. The results help guide treatment decisions and provide essential information for managing the condition. Diagnosing amyloidosis can be complex, and the cooperation of various healthcare professionals, including hematologists, nephrologists, and pathologists, may be required for an accurate and comprehensive assessment.

4.3 Imaging and Biopsy Procedures

In addition to laboratory tests and a thorough medical history, imaging and biopsy procedures play a crucial role in diagnosing amyloidosis. These procedures help confirm the presence of amyloid deposits, determine the extent of organ involvement, and establish the type of amyloidosis. Below, we discuss the common imaging and biopsy methods used in the diagnostic process.

Imaging Procedures

- **Echocardiogram**: An echocardiogram is a specialized ultrasound of the heart. It can reveal the presence of amyloid deposits in the heart muscle and assess the impact on cardiac function. Cardiac amyloidosis can lead to thickening of the heart walls, reduced cardiac output, and other abnormalities.

- **Electrocardiogram (ECG or EKG)**: An ECG records the electrical activity of the heart. It can identify irregular heart rhythms and conduction disturbances, which are common in cardiac amyloidosis.

- **Cardiac Magnetic Resonance Imaging (MRI)**: Cardiac MRI provides detailed images of the heart, offering insights into the heart's structure and function. It can be particularly useful in evaluating cardiac amyloidosis.

- **Computed Tomography (CT) Scan**: CT scans can detect amyloid deposits in various organs, such as the liver, spleen, kidneys, and gastrointestinal tract. It can also help assess bone involvement in certain forms of amyloidosis.

- **Magnetic Resonance Imaging (MRI)**: MRI scans may be performed to visualize organs and tissues affected by amyloidosis. They can provide detailed images and assess the extent of involvement.

- **Scintigraphy**: Nuclear medicine imaging techniques, such as bone scintigraphy with radiolabeled compounds like technetium-99m-pyrophosphate (99mTc-PYP), can be used to identify and quantify cardiac amyloid deposits.

Biopsy Procedures

- **Fat Pad Biopsy**: A fat pad biopsy is a relatively non-invasive procedure where a small sample of subcutaneous fat from the abdomen is taken. The fat tissue is examined under a microscope to identify amyloid deposits. This is a common initial diagnostic test for systemic amyloidosis, particularly AL amyloidosis.

- **Tissue Biopsy**: Depending on the suspected organ involvement, a tissue biopsy may be performed to directly sample affected tissues, such as the kidney, liver, gastrointestinal tract, or skin. The biopsy samples are examined under a microscope to confirm the presence of amyloid deposits and determine the type of amyloidosis.

- **Bone Marrow Biopsy**: In some cases, a bone marrow biopsy is performed to assess for underlying plasma cell disorders associated with AL amyloidosis. This may help identify the presence of monoclonal plasma cells and related disorders.

- **Endoscopic Procedures**: If the gastrointestinal tract is affected, endoscopic procedures, such as upper endoscopy or colonoscopy, can be used to obtain biopsies from the digestive tract.

- **Cardiac Biopsy**: In cases of suspected cardiac amyloidosis, a cardiac biopsy may be performed, usually during a heart procedure like a cardiac catheterization. This allows for the direct sampling of heart tissue for confirmation of amyloid deposits.

The choice of biopsy procedure depends on the clinical presentation, suspected organ involvement, and the type of amyloidosis being considered. Biopsies play a critical role in confirming the diagnosis and determining the type of amyloidosis. They also provide information for treatment planning and prognosis assessment.

CHAPTER 5

Types of Amyloidosis

5.1 Systemic Amyloidosis

Systemic amyloidosis is a category of amyloidosis that involves the widespread deposition of amyloid fibrils throughout multiple organs and tissues in the body. It is characterized by the systemic distribution of amyloid deposits, and different types of amyloid proteins can cause systemic amyloidosis. The most common forms of systemic amyloidosis include:

1. **AL Amyloidosis (Immunoglobulin Light Chain Amyloidosis):** AL amyloidosis is the most common form of systemic amyloidosis. It results from the abnormal deposition of immunoglobulin light chains, which are components of antibodies produced by plasma cells in the bone marrow. These misfolded light chains accumulate and form amyloid deposits in various organs, such as the heart, kidneys, liver, and nervous system. AL amyloidosis is often associated with plasma cell disorders, especially multiple myeloma.

2. **AA Amyloidosis (Amyloid A Amyloidosis):** AA amyloidosis is characterized by the deposition of amyloid A (AA) protein, which is an acute-phase reactant produced in response to chronic inflammatory conditions or infections. Chronic diseases like rheumatoid arthritis, Crohn's disease, and tuberculosis can trigger the production of AA protein, leading to its amyloid deposition in organs. AA amyloidosis primarily affects the kidneys, liver, and spleen.

3. **ATTR Amyloidosis (Transthyretin Amyloidosis):** ATTR amyloidosis is a systemic amyloidosis that is caused by the aggregation of transthyretin (TTR) protein. It

can be hereditary (hATTR) or acquired (wild-type or senile systemic). ATTR amyloidosis predominantly affects the heart, nervous system, and gastrointestinal tract. There are two main forms of hATTR amyloidosis: Val30Met and non-Val30Met, each associated with different genetic mutations.

4. **AApoAI and AApAII Amyloidosis:** These are rare forms of systemic amyloidosis caused by mutations in apolipoprotein AI (AApoAI) or apolipoprotein AII (AApoAII), leading to cardiac or kidney involvement, respectively.

5. **Senile Systemic Amyloidosis:** This type of systemic amyloidosis primarily affects

the heart and is more common in older individuals. It is associated with the deposition of TTR amyloid.

Systemic amyloidosis can affect multiple organs and systems, leading to a wide range of symptoms and complications. The specific presentation and prognosis can vary depending on the type of amyloidosis and the extent of organ involvement. Early diagnosis and a tailored treatment approach are critical for individuals with systemic amyloidosis to manage the disease and improve outcomes. The choice of treatment may depend on factors such as the type of amyloidosis, the organs affected, and the individual's overall health.

5.2 Localized Amyloidosis

Localized amyloidosis is a distinct category of amyloidosis characterized by the deposition of amyloid fibrils in specific organs or tissues without systemic involvement. Unlike systemic amyloidosis, which affects multiple organs throughout the body, localized amyloidosis typically remains confined to a single site. There are several types of localized amyloidosis, each associated with specific organ or tissue involvement:

1. **Localized Cutaneous Amyloidosis:** This form of amyloidosis primarily affects the skin. It can manifest as skin lesions, nodules, or plaques. While the condition is generally benign and non-life-threatening, it can cause

cosmetic concerns and discomfort. Common subtypes include macular amyloidosis and lichen amyloidosis.

2. **Localized Oral Amyloidosis:** Amyloid deposits may occur in the mouth, affecting the tongue, gums, and other oral tissues. This localized form can lead to difficulties in speaking and swallowing, but it is not typically associated with systemic disease.

3. **Localized Ocular (Eye) Amyloidosis:** Ocular amyloidosis can affect various parts of the eye, including the conjunctiva, cornea, and eyelids. It may result in symptoms like blurred vision or discomfort but usually doesn't involve other organs.

4. **Localized Respiratory Amyloidosis:** In some cases, amyloid deposits can accumulate in the respiratory tract, including the trachea, bronchi, or lung tissue. This localized form may lead to coughing, shortness of breath, or other respiratory symptoms.

5. **Localized Gastrointestinal Amyloidosis:** Amyloid deposits can occur in the digestive tract, causing localized symptoms such as abdominal pain, diarrhea, or constipation. The condition may affect the esophagus, stomach, or intestines.

6. **Localized Genitourinary Amyloidosis:** Amyloidosis can affect the urinary tract and genitalia, leading to symptoms

like urinary difficulties or genital swelling. Localized genitourinary amyloidosis is usually not associated with systemic disease.

Localized amyloidosis is generally considered less aggressive and less likely to lead to severe organ damage than systemic forms of the condition. However, the specific symptoms and complications can vary depending on the location of the amyloid deposits. Treatment options for localized amyloidosis may include local excision, laser therapy, or other procedures to manage symptoms or improve cosmetic appearance. In some cases, localized amyloidosis may resolve on its own without the need for intervention. It is essential to consult with healthcare professionals who are experienced in diagnosing and managing localized amyloidosis to determine the most appropriate approach for each individual case.

5.3 Hereditary Amyloidosis

Hereditary amyloidosis is a rare group of genetic disorders characterized by the inheritance of specific gene mutations that lead to the production of abnormal proteins and the subsequent deposition of amyloid fibrils in various organs and tissues. Unlike sporadic amyloidosis, which occurs without a known genetic cause, hereditary amyloidosis is directly linked to specific genetic mutations. There are several forms of hereditary amyloidosis, with each form associated with distinct genetic mutations and organ involvement:

1. **Hereditary Transthyretin Amyloidosis (hATTR):**
Hereditary transthyretin amyloidosis is one of the most well-known forms of hereditary amyloidosis. It results from mutations in the TTR gene, which encodes transthyretin (TTR) protein. TTR is primarily produced in the liver and plays a role in transporting thyroid hormone and vitamin A. Mutations in TTR can lead to the production of abnormal TTR protein, which forms amyloid deposits in various organs. hATTR amyloidosis can manifest as familial amyloid polyneuropathy (FAP) with nervous system involvement or familial amyloid cardiomyopathy

(FAC) with cardiac involvement.

2. **Hereditary Gelsolin Amyloidosis:** This rare form of hereditary amyloidosis results from mutations in the GSN gene, leading to the production of abnormal gelsolin protein. Gelsolin is involved in actin regulation and cell movement. Hereditary gelsolin amyloidosis primarily affects the eyes, skin, and nervous system.

3. **Hereditary Apolipoprotein AI Amyloidosis (hAApoAI):** hAApoAI amyloidosis is caused by mutations in the APOA1 gene, leading to the production of abnormal apolipoprotein AI (AApoAI) protein. AApoAI is involved in lipid metabolism. This form of

hereditary amyloidosis can result in cardiac amyloidosis.

4. **Hereditary Apolipoprotein AII Amyloidosis (hAApoAII):** hAApoAII amyloidosis is caused by mutations in the APOA2 gene, leading to the production of abnormal apolipoprotein AII (AApoAII) protein. AApoAII is involved in lipid metabolism. This form of hereditary amyloidosis primarily affects the kidneys, leading to renal amyloidosis.

Hereditary amyloidosis is typically passed down from one generation to the next, and the specific genetic mutations determine the type and severity of the condition. Symptoms and age of onset can vary, even among individuals with the same mutation. Due to its genetic basis, hereditary amyloidosis may be diagnosed through genetic testing, which can identify the presence of pathogenic mutations associated with the condition. Early diagnosis and genetic counseling are essential for individuals with a family history of hereditary amyloidosis. While there is no cure for hereditary amyloidosis, treatment options are available to manage symptoms, slow disease progression, and improve the quality of life for affected individuals.

CHAPTER 6

Treatment Options

6.1 Managing Amyloidosis

Managing amyloidosis involves a multifaceted approach aimed at controlling the disease, mitigating symptoms, and improving the quality of life for affected individuals. The specific management strategy varies depending on the type of amyloidosis, its severity, the organs involved, and the overall health of the patient. Here are key elements of managing amyloidosis:

1. **Identifying the Type and Extent of Amyloidosis:** A precise diagnosis is essential to guide treatment. Identifying the specific type of amyloidosis and the extent of organ involvement is crucial for tailoring the management plan.

2. **Treatment of Underlying Conditions:** In cases of secondary amyloidosis (AA amyloidosis), addressing the underlying chronic inflammatory or infectious disease is a critical component of management. Effective treatment of the underlying condition can help slow or halt the progression of amyloid deposits.

3. **Treatment for AL Amyloidosis**

(Immunoglobulin Light Chain Amyloidosis): AL amyloidosis, often associated with plasma cell disorders like multiple myeloma, requires a targeted approach. The primary treatment goal is to reduce the production of abnormal immunoglobulin light chains. Treatment options include:

- **Chemotherapy**: Chemotherapy regimens like bortezomib, cyclophosphamide, and dexamethasone (VCd) are commonly used to control the underlying plasma cell disorder.

- **Stem Cell Transplantation**: For eligible patients, high-dose chemotherapy followed by autologous stem cell transplantation can be considered.

4. **Treatment for ATTR Amyloidosis (Transthyretin Amyloidosis):** The management of ATTR amyloidosis depends on the specific type (hereditary or acquired) and the extent of organ involvement. Options may include:

- **TTR Stabilizers**: Medications like tafamidis and patisiran can stabilize the transthyretin protein, slowing the progression of the disease.

- **Liver Transplantation**: In hereditary TTR

amyloidosis, liver transplantation can replace the liver's production of mutant TTR with normal TTR from a donor.

- **Cardiac Medications**: Medications to manage heart symptoms may be prescribed for patients with cardiac involvement.

5. **Symptom Management:** Depending on the organs affected, patients may require medications and interventions to manage specific symptoms, such as diuretics for edema, pain management for neuropathy, and cardiac medications for heart-related issues.

6. **Supportive Care:** Complementary therapies and supportive care, such as physical therapy, speech therapy, and occupational therapy, can improve the quality of life for individuals with amyloidosis.

7. **Monitoring and Follow-Up:** Regular check-ups and monitoring of organ function are essential to track disease progression and treatment effectiveness. Adjustments to the treatment plan may be necessary based on how the disease evolves over time.

8. **Clinical Trials:** In some cases, individuals with amyloidosis may be eligible to participate in clinical trials to access experimental treatments and

contribute to advancing medical knowledge.

9. **Genetic Counseling:** For hereditary amyloidosis, genetic counseling is important for individuals and families to understand the genetic risk, inheritance pattern, and potential implications for family members.

10. **Diet and Lifestyle:** Dietary modifications and lifestyle changes, such as maintaining a heart-healthy diet, staying physically active, and avoiding alcohol, can help manage symptoms and support overall health.

Amyloidosis is a complex and rare condition, and the management plan should be developed in collaboration with healthcare professionals who have experience in treating the disease. Early diagnosis and prompt treatment can significantly improve outcomes and the overall prognosis for individuals with amyloidosis. The management approach is tailored to the specific needs and circumstances of each patient.

6.2 Medications and Therapies for Amyloidosis

The treatment of amyloidosis often involves a combination of medications and therapies aimed at addressing the underlying cause, managing symptoms, and slowing the progression of the disease. The choice of treatment depends on the type of amyloidosis and the organs affected.

Here are some key medications and therapies used in the management of amyloidosis:

1. Chemotherapy:

- **AL Amyloidosis:** Chemotherapy regimens, such as bortezomib, cyclophosphamide, and dexamethasone (VCd), are commonly used to target the underlying plasma cell disorder associated with AL amyloidosis. Other chemotherapy agents may also be considered based on the individual's condition.

2. Stem Cell Transplantation:

- **AL Amyloidosis:** Autologous stem cell transplantation, often combined with high-dose chemotherapy, may be recommended for eligible patients with AL amyloidosis. This procedure aims to replace diseased bone marrow with healthy stem cells.

3. TTR Stabilizers:

- **ATTR Amyloidosis:** Medications like tafamidis and patisiran can stabilize the transthyretin (TTR) protein in hereditary ATTR amyloidosis. By preventing the misfolding of TTR, these drugs can slow disease progression.

4. Heart Medications:

- **Cardiac Amyloidosis:** Medications such as beta-blockers, angiotensin-converting enzyme (ACE) inhibitors, angiotensin receptor blockers (ARBs), and diuretics may be prescribed to manage heart symptoms in individuals with cardiac amyloidosis.

5. Pain Management:

- **Neuropathy:** Pain management techniques, including analgesic medications and nerve-specific medications, can help alleviate neuropathic pain associated with amyloidosis.

6. Diuretics:

- **Edema:** Diuretics may be prescribed to manage fluid retention (edema), which is common in amyloidosis patients, especially those with cardiac or renal involvement.

7. Supportive Therapies:

- **Physical Therapy:** Physical therapy can improve mobility and strength, particularly for individuals with amyloidosis-related neuropathy or musculoskeletal problems.

- **Occupational Therapy:** Occupational therapy focuses on helping individuals maintain independence in daily activities despite physical limitations.

- **Speech Therapy:** For those with speech and swallowing difficulties due to amyloid deposits in the throat or vocal cords, speech therapy can be beneficial.

8. Liver Transplantation:

- **Hereditary ATTR Amyloidosis:** In cases of hereditary ATTR amyloidosis where the liver is the primary source of mutant TTR, liver transplantation can replace the liver's production of abnormal TTR with healthy TTR from a donor.

9. Organ-Specific Interventions:

- **Gastrointestinal Amyloidosis:** Interventions such as endoscopy or surgery may be required to manage gastrointestinal complications.

- **Renal Amyloidosis:** Treatment may involve medications to manage kidney complications or, in severe cases, dialysis or kidney transplantation.

10. Clinical Trials:

- Participation in clinical trials offers access to experimental treatments and contributes to advancing our understanding of amyloidosis and its management.

It's important to work closely with a healthcare team that specializes in amyloidosis to develop a comprehensive treatment plan tailored to the individual's specific type of amyloidosis, organ involvement, and overall health. Regular monitoring and follow-up are crucial to assess the response to treatment and make adjustments as needed. Genetic counseling may also be recommended for individuals with hereditary amyloidosis to address genetic risk and implications for family members.

6.3 Potential Complications of Amyloidosis

Amyloidosis is a complex disease that can lead to a range of potential complications, especially when left untreated or undiagnosed. The specific complications can vary depending on the type of amyloidosis and the organs affected. Here are some of the common potential complications associated with amyloidosis:

1. **Organ Dysfunction:** One of the primary complications of amyloidosis is organ dysfunction. As amyloid deposits accumulate in various organs, they disrupt their normal structure and function. This can lead to a wide range of

complications, such as heart failure, kidney damage, liver dysfunction, gastrointestinal problems, and more, depending on the specific organs involved.

2. **Cardiac Complications:** Cardiac amyloidosis can result in complications such as heart arrhythmias, restrictive cardiomyopathy, heart failure, and sudden cardiac death. It can also lead to other cardiovascular issues like orthostatic hypotension and difficulty in maintaining blood pressure.

3. **Kidney Damage:** Renal amyloidosis can cause kidney damage and lead to proteinuria (excess protein in the urine), nephrotic syndrome, and

kidney failure if not managed properly.

4. **Neuropathy:** Amyloidosis can cause peripheral neuropathy, which can lead to sensory and motor deficits, including numbness, tingling, muscle weakness, and difficulty with fine motor skills.

5. **Gastrointestinal Problems:** Gastrointestinal amyloidosis can result in complications like malabsorption, diarrhea, constipation, and gastrointestinal bleeding.

6. **Orthopedic Complications:** Amyloid deposits in bones and joints can lead to pain, joint stiffness, and restricted mobility.

7. **Skin Issues:** In some cases, skin lesions, nodules, or plaques can develop, affecting the appearance and comfort of individuals with amyloidosis.

8. **Respiratory Complications:** Amyloid deposits in the respiratory tract may cause coughing, shortness of breath, and other respiratory symptoms.

9. **Eye Involvement:** Ocular amyloidosis can lead to eye problems, including keratoconjunctivitis, dry eyes, and visual disturbances.

10. **Bleeding Disorders:** Amyloidosis can lead to bleeding disorders, including easy bruising, nosebleeds, and gastrointestinal bleeding due to

amyloid deposits interfering with blood clotting.

11. **Risk of Amyloidosis in Transplanted Organs:** In rare cases, individuals with systemic amyloidosis who receive organ transplants, such as kidney or liver transplants, can experience amyloid deposits in the transplanted organ.

12. **Systemic Complications:** Systemic amyloidosis can affect multiple organs and systems throughout the body, leading to a wide range of symptoms and complications, including fatigue, weight loss, and edema.

13. **Infections:** Amyloid deposits can compromise the function of affected organs and may make

individuals more susceptible to infections.

It's important to note that the severity and combination of these complications can vary widely between individuals and are influenced by the type of amyloidosis, the extent of organ involvement, and the stage of the disease. Timely diagnosis, appropriate treatment, and close medical monitoring are essential to manage and reduce these complications. Comprehensive care from a team of healthcare professionals experienced in amyloidosis is critical to address the specific needs of each individual with the condition.

6.4 Coping Strategies for Living with Amyloidosis

Amyloidosis is a rare and complex disease that can significantly impact an individual's life. Coping with amyloidosis involves addressing not only the physical symptoms but also the emotional and psychosocial challenges that the condition can bring. Here are some coping strategies to help individuals living with amyloidosis:

1. **Educate Yourself:**
   Understanding amyloidosis and its specific type is essential. Knowledge empowers individuals to actively participate in their care, ask informed questions, and make decisions about their treatment.

2. **Build a Support Network:** Connect with family, friends, and support groups to share experiences and concerns. Support from loved ones can be invaluable in navigating the challenges of amyloidosis.

3. **Seek Specialized Care:** Ensure that you receive care from healthcare professionals experienced in treating amyloidosis. A multidisciplinary team may include hematologists, nephrologists, cardiologists, and other specialists depending on the organ involvement.

4. **Follow Treatment Plans:** Adherence to your treatment plan is crucial. This may include medications, therapies, and lifestyle modifications.

Regular check-ups and follow-up appointments are essential to monitor your progress.

5. **Manage Symptoms:** Work with your healthcare team to manage and alleviate specific symptoms. This may involve pain management, physical therapy, and medications to control complications like edema or neuropathy.

6. **Emotional Support:** Dealing with a rare and potentially serious disease can be emotionally challenging. Seek emotional support from professionals or support groups to help cope with feelings of anxiety, depression, or stress.

7. **Genetic Counseling:** If you have hereditary amyloidosis,

genetic counseling can provide guidance on family planning, inheritance, and the potential risk to family members.

8. **Diet and Lifestyle:** Maintain a balanced diet and stay physically active within your limits. Avoid alcohol and tobacco, as they can exacerbate amyloidosis symptoms.

9. **Balance Rest and Activity:** Listen to your body and find a balance between rest and activity. Fatigue is common in amyloidosis, so pacing yourself and conserving energy is important.

10. **Advance Directives:** Consider discussing and documenting your healthcare preferences, especially if you are in

advanced stages of amyloidosis. Advance directives can help ensure that your wishes are respected.

11. **Set Realistic Goals:** Amyloidosis can be a chronic condition, and managing expectations is crucial. Set achievable goals for yourself, focusing on improving your quality of life.

12. **Advocate for Yourself:** Be an active advocate for your health. Ask questions, seek second opinions, and communicate openly with your healthcare team about your concerns and goals.

13. **Participate in Clinical Trials:** Depending on your circumstances, you may be

eligible to participate in clinical trials, which can provide access to cutting-edge treatments and contribute to advancing medical knowledge.

14. **Live in the Present:** While managing amyloidosis is important, it's equally important to enjoy life in the present moment. Engage in activities and spend time with loved ones that bring you joy.

Amyloidosis affects individuals differently, and what works best for one person may not be the same for another. Tailor your coping strategies to your unique circumstances, and don't hesitate to seek professional guidance and support when needed. Living with amyloidosis can be challenging, but with the right strategies and a strong support system, it is possible to manage the condition and improve your overall well-being.

6.5 The Importance of Early Detection of Amyloidosis

Early detection of amyloidosis is critical for several reasons, as it can significantly impact the prognosis and quality of life for individuals affected by this rare and complex disease. Here are key reasons why early detection is crucial:

1. **Effective Treatment:** Many types of amyloidosis, such as AL amyloidosis and ATTR amyloidosis, benefit from early intervention. Prompt diagnosis allows for the initiation of

treatment strategies that can slow or halt the progression of the disease. Early treatment can lead to better outcomes and potentially a higher quality of life.

2. **Prevention of Organ Damage:** Amyloid deposits in various organs can lead to irreversible damage if left untreated. Early detection and management can help prevent or minimize the extent of organ damage, particularly in the heart, kidneys, liver, and nervous system.

3. **Symptom Relief:** Amyloidosis can cause a wide range of symptoms, from fatigue and edema to heart problems and neuropathy. Early diagnosis allows for symptom

management and can improve the individual's overall well-being and comfort.

4. **Improving Quality of Life:** Managing amyloidosis early in the disease course can help individuals maintain a higher level of function and quality of life. This includes addressing symptoms, managing complications, and preserving organ function.

5. **Tailored Treatment Plans:** Early diagnosis enables healthcare professionals to develop personalized treatment plans based on the specific type of amyloidosis, the extent of organ involvement, and the individual's overall health. Tailored approaches are more

effective in managing the disease.

6. **Identification of Underlying Conditions:** Amyloidosis can be secondary to other underlying conditions, such as chronic inflammatory diseases. Early detection of amyloidosis can lead to the identification and treatment of these underlying diseases, addressing the root cause of amyloid production.

7. **Genetic Counseling:** In hereditary forms of amyloidosis, early detection allows for genetic counseling to assess the risk to family members and provide guidance on family planning and screening.

8. **Clinical Trials:** Early detection may make individuals eligible to participate in clinical trials, offering access to experimental treatments that can potentially improve outcomes and advance medical knowledge.

9. **Avoiding Misdiagnosis:** The symptoms of amyloidosis can overlap with those of other conditions, leading to misdiagnosis. Early detection helps prevent misdiagnosis and ensures that the appropriate diagnostic tests are conducted.

10. **Enhanced Survival Rates:** When amyloidosis is detected at an earlier stage, individuals have a better chance of achieving longer-term survival. The prognosis for amyloidosis is generally more favorable

when the disease is diagnosed and treated early.

Given that amyloidosis is a rare condition and its symptoms can mimic those of other more common diseases, early detection can be challenging. However, healthcare professionals, especially those experienced in the field of amyloidosis, play a crucial role in recognizing the disease and conducting the necessary diagnostic tests. If you or someone you know experiences unexplained symptoms or has a family history of amyloidosis, seeking medical attention and discussing the possibility of amyloidosis is essential for early detection and timely intervention.

Made in the USA
Middletown, DE
21 October 2024